TWELVE MEN OF ACTION
in Graeco-Roman History

TWELVE MEN OF ACTION
in Graeco-Roman History

translated with an introduction by
ARNOLD J. TOYNBEE

THE BEACON PRESS · BOSTON

Seeing we also are compassed about with so great a cloud of witnesses. . . .

HEBREWS 12: 1

Contents

Introduction

The sketches here reproduced from the original Greek give no adequate idea of the portrait gallery from which they are drawn. Their purpose is to tantalize the reader into entering the building himself and exploring the treasures of its vast interior. The present translator's problem has been how to select and where to stop. He has found it difficult not to swell this little book into a substantial volume by taking one brilliant picture after another out of the pages of Plutarch. Plutarch's *Parallel Lives,* as even this anthology will show, are by no means our only extant source for the biography of the Graeco-Roman world; yet consider, for a moment, the enormous influence upon our modern Western world of Plutarch's work alone — its influence, for example, upon Shakespeare's choice of plots or upon the sentiment, and even upon the course, of the French Revolution. Yet Plutarch himself would have been the first to admit that his *Lives* were mere "crumbs from the mighty banquet" of Hellenic biographical literature — a branch of the classics which has been lost to us almost completely in its original form.[1] Plutarch's *Lives*, in fact, are "potted" lives (though the most academic-minded man of letters would be proud to have been the author of such masterpieces) and, further, they are practically confined to men of action. Had Plutarch included artists, poets, philosophers, and scientists in his series, he would probably have broken the back of his publisher — even though he had exerted all his art to keep his work upon its actual miniature scale. So great was the cloud of witnesses that compassed about the later generations of a Hellenic society.

The present "fragments of fragments" have been selected more for their human interest than for their historical importance (though all of them are flotsam on the main stream of history), and this explains why Clearchus, Proxenus, and Meno are presented while Alexander and Caesar fail to appear. It may be useful to conclude with a word or two upon each individual.

Themistocles is the first great man of action in Hellenic

---

[1] This is one of the most deplorable gaps in our knowledge of ancient Greek literature. The reason is that most of the great biographies were written during the period between the conquests of Alexander the Great and the establishment of the Roman Empire (334 B.C.-31 B.C.) and were therefore naturally composed in the special style of their age. Under the Empire, however, taste turned sharply against this "Asiatic" style and deliberately reverted to the "Attic" models of the preceding century (431-334 B.C.). The prejudice was carried to such lengths that the voluminous but thenceforth unfashionable literature of the intervening period was allowed to pass out of circulation and was only preserved in so far as it happened to be worked over (often for the worse) into the style affected by the representatives of "the Attic Revival."

history of whose individuality some record is preserved.

Pericles worthily represents the most inspired generation of the Athenians, who were themselves the greatest [2]
nation in the Graeco-Roman world.

The sketch of Cyrus shows how a contemporary Hellene, who was himself a man of action and a man of
letters in one, could appreciate the noble elements in the
rival and to some extent antipathetic contemporary civilization of the Middle East; while the Hellenic *condottieri*
serving under Cyrus's banner illustrate various psycho-
logical reactions to the first Hellenic "World War"[3]
which are particularly interesting to us in age.

Cleomenes the Last and his companions (both women
and men) were the quintessence of that spirit which had
made the Spartans a "peculiar people" during the preceding three or four hundred years — and this at the
moment when Sparta, Athens, Thebes, and the other
city-states of "mediaeval" Hellas were being overwhelmed
by new great powers of the caliber of Macedon, Seleucid
Asia, Egypt, Carthage, and Rome — much as Milan,
Florence, Venice, Ghent, Bruges, Nuremberg, Frankfort,
and the other city-states of the mediaeval West were
overwhelmed, in the sixteenth century after Christ, by
the new great powers of the modern Western world,
and as these, in their turn, are now being overwhelmed
by the United States and the Soviet Union.

---

[2] Greatest, but not largest and certainly not militarily strongest,
except for a brief period of seventy-three years (478-405 B.C.).

[3] The Peloponnesian War (431-404 B.C.).

Cato the Elder embodies Rome, one of these fresh actors on the stage, at the moment when she was Hellenizing herself and was simultaneously asserting her predominance over that now ancient Hellenic society of which she was the youngest and the crudest member. As the hard, willful, capable barbarian who has assimilated this and that from a civilization not his own, Cato has in him a touch of old Prince Bolkonsky in Tolstoy's *War and Peace,* while Americans or Continental Europeans might see in him a prototype of "British hypocrisy." Cato, who was taken in by nobody but himself, deserves all the irony which he lavished upon others. Starting life as an old-fashioned yeoman-farmer, he fancied himself in that character until the end of his days, though actually he became a "self-made" man who had forced his way into the ranks of the "new rich" by mastering and applying the "scientific management" of the Carthaginian plantations and the "business methods" of Egyptian and Asiatic high finance. Posing, again, as a Philistine, he perhaps accomplished more than any other Roman of his time (and this is immensely to his credit) toward making the Latin language a vehicle for Hellenic culture. Pursuing, lastly, a successful career as a practical statesman, he utterly failed to grasp the needs or to hear the prayers of a world left in ruins by the second "World War" of Graeco-Roman history.[4] Cato emerged as a young man from that awful ordeal not only materially

---

[4] The Hannibalic War (218-201 B.C.).

but spiritually unscathed. In all senses of that odious term he was a "war profiteer" — and yet the reader will agree that he compels us into liking him in spite of ourselves!

Scipio the Younger exemplifies the rapid progress of Hellenism at Rome after the lapse of a single generation, while his intimacy with Polybius, the statesman and historian in exile from Megalopolis in the Peloponnese, reveals one point of contact through which the gracious influences of civilization were conducted.

Finally, we watch the last hours of Cato the Younger, whose contrast to his celebrated ancestor gives us a measure of the difference, not only between the personal characters of the two men, but between the circumstances of their respective ages. In the Younger Cato's generation, the sins of the fathers were visited — and that with interest — upon the children; and it was because the Elder Cato had died in his bed, with a good conscience in his brainpan and a good balance in his ledger, that his descendant was doomed to die by his own sword at Utica, with the iron piercing through the flesh into the soul. In the person of Cato the Younger the Roman had become a Hellene through and through. The antique patriotism of the city-state and the modern individualism of the Stoic philosophy, which inspired him in unison, together constituted the essence of the Hellenic civilization in his day. Yet Cato's soul was almost the last in which action and faith retained the equilibrium in which they had been held successfully for four tense centuries. The obverse to Cato's tragedy was the establishment of the Roman Empire, and under the Empire the men of faith became more and more dominant, until the great catastrophe in which the Graeco-Roman civilization went to pieces forced them to be their brothers' keepers in the Valley of the Shadow of Death.

Thus Cato closes one series of Titanic figures only to open another which leads on to Augustine of Madaura, Benedict of Nursia, and Gregory the Great — and these in turn were the primaeval creators of our own Western world. "Let us now praise famous men and our fathers that begat us" — but that is another story.

A. J. T.

THEMISTOCLES

THEMISTOCLES

525-459 B.C.

From Thucydides, Book I, Chaps. 93, 135-138.

Themistocles

Thanks to Themistocles' diplomacy,[1] the Athenians fortified their town at short notice, and to this day the building preserves the marks of the haste with which it was done. The foundations are composed of miscellaneous stones which in places are not even fitted, but are laid just as they came, while a number of tombstones and dressed blocks have been worked into this masonry. The circuit was extended in every direction, and for this reason they laid hands indiscriminately on everything that could help them to push forward.

Themistocles also persuaded them to finish the construction of the Piraeus, which he had begun during his year of public office. He was struck by the advantages of the place with its three natural harbors, and was convinced that a maritime career was Athens' avenue to power. In fact he was the first who ventured to say that she must take to the sea. His plans for the Piraeus were an integral part of his empire-building, and, on his motion, they constructed the walls of the port on the scale

---

[1] The reference is to the (possibly apocryphal) story of an incident alleged to have occurred immediately after the Persian War and recorded just previously by the author. [Ed.]

which anyone can see for himself today. They were made broad enough for two trains of wagons to cross one another as they brought up the stones, while in the interior there was no rubble or mortar but great squared blocks fitted and morticed together with iron and lead clamps on the outer surfaces to bond them. The height to which these walls were carried, however, was only about half what Themistocles had planned. He wanted them to be so broad and so high as to make it hopeless for an enemy to attempt them, his idea being that they could be garrisoned by a small force consisting of the least fit, leaving the rest of the country's man power available for the navy. The navy came first in his thoughts — I imagine because he had observed that the great Persian expedition was more successful in its operations by sea than in those by land. He also considered the Piraeus a better site than the upper city, and he often advised his countrymen, if ever they were outmatched on land, to throw themselves into the Piraeus and hold out with their navy against the world. . . .

When Pausanias [2] had met his fate, the Lacedaemonians sent a note to Athens implicating Themistocles in the same treasonable relations with Persia. Evidence against him had come out in the exposure of Pausanias, and they demanded that he should receive the same sentence. The Athenians agreed; and, since Themistocles happened to

---

[2] Commander of the allied Greek forces at Plataea and Regent of Sparta for his cousin King Plistarchus, who was a minor. [ED.]

be temporarily banished from Athens and had made his headquarters at Argos,[3] the Athenian government attached representatives of their own to the Lacedaemonian mission (who were prepared to lend their assistance) with instructions to arrest him wherever found. Warned in time, Themistocles fled from the Peloponnese to Corcyra, a power which was under an obligation to him; but the Corcyraeans declared that they dared not incur the displeasure of Lacedaemon and Athens by keeping him, and they convoyed him to the opposite mainland.

The pursuivants were hot upon his tracks; and, finding himself in a tight corner, he was forced to seek shelter with King Admetus of the Molossians, who was far from being his friend. The King happened to be away, and the Queen, on whose mercy the fugitive had thrown himself, instructed him to take his seat at the hearth with their child in his arms. When Admetus came home, as he did soon afterwards, Themistocles revealed his identity and appealed to him not to take revenge on him now for having once opposed some application of the King's in the Athenian Assembly. In his present plight he would be an easy prey, while revenge could be taken by a man of honor only from his peers and upon equal terms; besides which, he (Themistocles) had opposed the King, not on a question of life and death, but on some point of secondary interest, while the King, in extraditing Themistocles (he here explained the facts of his position), would vir-

---

[3] From which center he was touring the Peloponnese. [AUTHOR.]

tually be condemning him to death. After listening to him, the King raised him to his feet with the King's son still in his arms;[4] and, when, not long afterwards, the Lacedaemonian and Athenian mission arrived, he refused to give him up, in spite of their energetic representations. Instead, he, sent him off overland to the Macedonian port of Pydna on the opposite coast of the peninsula — his eventual goal being Persia.

At Pydna, Themistocles took passage on a merchant-man bound for Ionia, and was carried by a gale into the arms of the Athenian force besieging Naxos. In this crisis he abandoned the incognito which he had hitherto maintained on board, told the captain who he was and why he was in his present position, and threatened to declare that he (the captain) had been bribed to take him on board unless he managed to save the situation. The only salvation, he added, would be for no one to leave the ship until the voyage could be continued, and, if the captain did what he asked, he would know how to reward him. The captain did as he was told, rode out the storm for a day and a night in the offing, and subsequently arrived at Ephesus.

After gratifying the captain with a present of money,[5] he traveled to the interior in the company of a provincial grandee, and sent in a memorial to King Artaxerxes, who

---

[4] A powerful appeal according to the local code of chivalry. [AUTHOR.]

[5] Funds reached him eventually from friends in Athens and from his deposit in Argos. [AUTHOR.]

had recently succeeded his father Xerxes on the throne of Persia. The sense of this document was as follows:

"Your Majesty's humble petitioner is Themistocles, who did your dynasty more damage than any single man in Hellas, so long as he was forced to defend himself against the attacks of Your Majesty's imperial father, while he afterwards performed even greater services, as soon as the tables were turned and the safety of Your Majesty's imperial father's retreat was threatened. Your petitioner has a benefaction to his credit;[6] and, now that he has arrived at Your Majesty's court, after being cast out by his countrymen for his devotion to Your Majesty, he is in a position to do you valuable services. He begs for a year's grace before presenting himself in person to explain the objects of his mission."

The Emperor is reported to have been impressed by his cleverness and to have granted his request. Themistocles employed his year's grace in mastering the Persian language and Persian deportment to the best of his ability, presented himself at court at the end of the period, and rose to what for a Hellene was an unprecedented position there, owing partly to his established prestige, partly to the hopes which he held out of bringing Hellas into subjection to the Emperor, but principally to the practiced proofs which he gave of his ability.

---

[6] Here he mentioned the warning to retire, which he had sent to Xerxes from Salamis, and his (quite fictitious) instrumentality in subsequently saving the bridges over the Dardanelles. [AUTHOR.]

Themistocles was, in fact, an unmistakable genius, head and shoulders above any other claimant to the title. Though his native ability was neither formed nor supplemented by study, he possessed a marvelous intuitive judgment in emergencies and a vision that penetrated unerringly to distant horizons of the future. He possessed the gift of exposition as well as the gift for affairs, and his critical faculties did not desert him in matters outside the range of his personal experience. His eye for hidden potentialities, good or evil, was uncannily piercing. In a word he stands out, with his brilliant but almost untrained natural endowments, as an unrivaled master of successful improvisation.

PERICLES

PERICLES

c. 495-429 B.C.

From Thucydides, Book II, Chap. 65.

Pericles

The object of Pericles' apologia was to appease his countrymen's anger against himself and to divert their minds from the ills of the moment. Politically they were sufficiently convinced to put fresh energy into the war instead of making further overtures to the Lacedaemonians. Privately, however, their sufferings filled them with resentment. The masses found themselves deprived of the little that they had ever possessed, while the upper class felt the loss of their fine estates in the country, with their buildings and other lavish capital investments;[1] but the fundamental grievance was the exchange of peace for war. In fact, the collective anger against Pericles was not appeased until he had been condemned to pay a fine, and then, at a short interval, they displayed the characteristic

---

[1] This feeling is reflected in the contemporary plays of Aristophanes, but the devastation of Attica at this stage was much less serious than it came to be during the second phase of the war (414-404 B.C.). That later stage is described in the following fragment of an unknown Hellenic historian, which was recovered in the present century on papyrus No. 842 from Oxyrrhynchus in Egypt, *Oxyrrhynchia cum Theopompi et Cratippi Fragmentis: Hellenica* (Oxford text, ed. by B. P. Grenfell and A. S. Hunt): "Thebes made another important advance in prosperity from the time when she joined Lacedaemon in establishing a hostile post at Decelea in Athenian territory. The slaves and all

psychology of the crowd by electing him to office and giving him a free hand — the explanation being that their private grievances had begun to lose their edge, while Pericles' political reputation for the conduct of public affairs stood as high as ever.

Indeed, his moderate and cautious statesmanship during the period before the war had given Athens the greatest epoch in her history, and when the war broke out he displayed equal ability in gauging her power. He survived the outbreak of hostilities by two years and six months, and the correctness of his forecast had obtained general recognition by the time of his death. He prophesied the victory of Athens on condition that she remained on the defensive, kept up her navy, resisted the temptation to extend her possessions till the war was over, and took no gambler's risks. His warnings, however, were disobeyed on every point, and the country (to its own and its allies' undoing) was committed by private ambitions and interests to enterprises obviously extraneous to the war, which would have redounded mainly to the glory and gain of individuals if they had succeeded,

other prizes of war were taken over by the Thebans at a low price, while the fact that their frontiers marched with those of Athens enabled them to transport into their own territory all the fruits of the capital invested in Attica, down to the beams and tiles from the houses. At that period, capital had been invested in the Athenian countryside more lavishly than in any other country in Hellas, and the damage inflicted by the Lacedaemonians in their previous invasions had been too trifling to counterbalance the incomparably elaborate and intensive improvements that had been carried out by the Athenians." [Ed.]

and which proved so many military disasters to the country when they came to grief.

The explanation lies in the contrast between Pericles and his successors. Pericles' rank, ability, and conspicuous integrity placed him in a position to exercise an independent control over the masses. So far from being led, he was the leader, because he was not tempted into flattery by any improprieties in his political career, but enjoyed a reputation which could brave the storms of unpopularity. Whenever he saw his countrymen unseasonably and insolently elated, he could bring them to their senses by a word, and when they were irrationally alarmed he was equally successful in restoring their confidence. A nominal democracy became in his hands a government by the dominant personality.

His successors were more nearly on a level with one another, and their competition for the dominant position led them to flatter the people by abandoning control to them. This exposed Athens to all the blunders that can be committed by a great imperial power, culminating in the expedition to Sicily; and that enterprise failed not so much through a miscalculation of the enemy's strength as through the egotism of the politicians, who neglected the interests of the expeditionary force in their personal intrigues for office, and thus not only produced paralysis at the front, but sowed the seeds of civil disorder at home. Their losses in Sicily included the greater part of their fleet, while at home they had by that time lost their national unity. Yet they held out ten years longer against their original opponents reinforced from Sicily, against the majority of their own allies who had revolted, and against the Emperor's son Cyrus,[2] who afterwards joined the coalition and financed the Peloponnesian fleet; and they did not give in till they had brought destruction on their own heads by their internal dissensions. The width of the margin thus revealed in Pericles' calculations would have given Athens an easy victory over the Peloponnesians by themselves.

_____

[2] Cyrus the Younger, son of Emperor Darius II of Persia. [ED.]

CYRUS THE YOUNGER

CYRUS THE YOUNGER

c. 425-401 B.C.

From Xenophon, *Cyrus' Expedition*, Book I, Chap. 9.

Cyrus the Younger

The death of Cyrus deprived the Persian nation of its noblest representative since the days of his namesake Cyrus the Elder. His kingliness and his gift for leadership are acknowledged by every observer who can claim to have come into personal contact with him, and these qualities revealed themselves at an early age. In his first phase, when he was being educated with his brother and the other boys, he was felt to excel all his companions in every field. All the sons of the Persian nobility are educated "at the King's Doors" — an admirable school for character, where nothing ignoble can reach the scholars' eyes or ears. The boys learn by eye and ear how some parties are honored by the King and how others are treated with dishonor — an experience which instructs them, from their youth up, in the secrets of leadership and subordination. In this school, Cyrus enjoyed the double reputation of being the most gentlemanly of his contemporaries — a boy who showed greater deference towards his elders than was actually shown by his inferiors — as well as being the keenest and the best rider of them all. He was also awarded the palm for eagerness to learn and willingness to take pains in the military exercises of archery and the *jerid*.[1]

Later, when he reached the age, he became an enthusiastic hunter and, what is more, a daring sportsman in pursuit of big game. Once, when charged by a bear, he did not flinch but grappled with the animal, was dragged off his horse, and suffered injuries — of which he ever afterwards bore the scars — before he finally succeeded in putting it out of action.[2] Later again, when he was sent out by his father [3] to take over the governor-generalship of Lydia, Greater Phrygia, and Cappadocia,[4] and was appointed military commander of all the feudal militia whose place of rendezvous was the Plain of Castolus,[5] his first concern was to leave no doubt about his absolute determination to observe every treaty, compact, and promise of his to the letter. Actually, the autonomous states in his province used to place themselves confidently in his hands, and individuals used to do the same; while anyone who had been at war with him was always confident, when once Cyrus had made peace, that there

---

[1] A Persian sport, consisting of a kind of tournament of javelin-throwing on horseback, which remained a favorite amusement among the Osmanlis and other Oriental peoples down to the recent introduction of Western manners among them. [ED.]

[2] I ought to mention that he showered rewards upon the fortunate huntsman who first came to his assistance. [AUTHOR.]

[3] Emperor Darius II. [ED.]

[4] Approximately coextensive with the Ottoman province of Aydin, Qoniyeh, Sivas, and Qaysari. [ED.]

[5] Corresponding to the former Ottoman Beglerbeglik of Anadolu. [ED.]

would be no violation of the treaty. Accordingly, when he went to war with Tissaphernes,[6] all the autonomous states of their own accord transferred their allegiance from Tissaphernes to the Prince with the exception of Miletus; and the Milesians were afraid of Cyrus only because he refused to throw over their exiles.

It was always Cyrus' patent endeavor to repay every good turn and every bad turn with interest. In fact, there was current a story of his making it his prayer that his life might be spared until he had more than requited those who had done him good and evil. Certainly no single individual in our generation could boast so many admirers eager to sacrifice fortune, country, and life itself in his cause; while at the same time nobody could maintain that Cyrus permitted criminals and lawbreakers to defy him, for he was as ruthless as anybody in bringing them to book. Footless, handless, and eyeless victims of his justice were common roadside spectacles along the highways, with the result that, within the limits of Cyrus' province, any law-abiding person, Hellene or Oriental, could travel in security wherever he chose, and could reap the rewards of his labors.

Cyrus' principal attentions, however, were admittedly bestowed upon military qualities. He begun by making war upon the Pisidians and Mysians;[7] and, through taking

---

[6] The previous incumbent of the Persian province of Lydia, corresponding to the Ottoman province of Aydin. [ED.]

[7] Two groups of unpacificated tribesmen within the boundaries of his command. The Mysians lived among the mountains of

a personal part in these campaigns, he was able to pick out the officers who were not afraid of risking their lives, whom he placed in command of the conquered districts as a step toward further promotion. This established the principle that bravery was the avenue to a career, and servitude to the brave the destiny of the coward; and accordingly Cyrus could always count upon a keen competition among his soldiers to risk life and limb in his cause, whenever the action was likely to come under the Prince's notice.

Honesty, again, was encouraged in the army by Cyrus' absolute determination to ensure that officers who displayed a devotion to this virtue should be materially better off than those who were not above making dishonest profits. Honesty was Cyrus' principle in every department of administration, and the result was that he had a genuine army at his command. Generals and company commanders whose motive in joining him had been mercenary discovered that there was more money in the performance of distinguished service for Cyrus than in their monthly profits. The fact was that no soldier ever performed distinguished service in execution of Cyrus' orders without finding his zeal well rewarded; and because of this it became a byword that Cyrus was incomparably served in every conceivable enterprise. Whenever he

---

Simav, on the borderline between the provinces of Aydin and Brusa, while the Pisidians occupied the mountain triangle between Mughla, Egirdir, and Adalia, on the border between the provinces of Aydin and Qoniyeh. [ED.]

noticed a clever, and at the same time honest, administrator who knew how to organize his district and to raise revenue, he never thought of squeezing him but invariably gave him a bonus, with the result that people not only worked for Cyrus cheerfully but made money fearlessly, and that it rarely occurred to anyone to conceal from Cyrus the fortune that he had accumulated, because the Prince made it obvious that he had no ill will toward wealth openly displayed and only attempted to avail himself of funds when the possessors were secretive.

In the matter of friendship, again, whenever Cyrus made a friend and was sure of his devotion and judged him capable of assisting him in the accomplishment of any particular purpose, he is universally admitted to have been without a match in treating that friend as a true friend deserves. Just as, on his own side, he valued his friends as so many potential assistants, so he set himself to be an incomparable assistant to his friends for the attainment of whatever he saw to be their respective ambitions.

As for presents, I imagine that no single individual ever received so many as, for a number of reasons, were received by Cyrus, and his chief use for such presents was to distribute them among his friends — always with an eye to their idiosyncrasies and to their most pressing individual needs. Among the presents which he used to receive were clothes and arms and *objets de luxe,* and in regard to all these there was current a saying of his to the effect that his own person could not possibly be adorned with all these articles, but that he conceived a gentleman's best adornment to be that of his friends. The vast material disparity of the interest with which he returned his friends' attentions was not particularly surprising, considering the vastly greater means at his disposal; but the way in which he surpassed his friends in taking pains and showing genuine concern in order to give pleasure was, to my mind, something really wonderful. For example, he would often send half-decanted bottles of wine, whenever he had found a particularly fine vintage, with a message that it had been ever so long since he had hit upon a finer wine than this. Often, again, he would send a half-finished goose or a broken loaf or some other trifle, with orders to the bearer to add the message: "Cyrus found these good, so he wishes you too to taste them." Or, again, whenever there was a serious scarcity of fodder and when Cyrus had succeeded in obtaining some for himself owing to the number of his personal staff and to their good organization, he would send round loads of it, asking his friends to accept this fodder as feed for their own mounts, in order that no friend of his might have to ride a starving animal.

Whenever he was on a progress and was most under the public eye, he used to call his friends to his side and to enter into serious conversation with them, in order to make it clear who enjoyed his esteem; and personally I should say, from what I hear, that nobody has ever been beloved more universally by Hellenes and Orientals without distinction. There is evidence of this in the fact that, with a single exception,[8] none offered to desert from Cyrus, the Emperor's slave, to the Emperor, while numbers deserted from the Emperor to Cyrus as soon as the two found themselves at war — the deserters being actually the Emperor's chief favorites — because they expected that meritorious service with Cyrus would be rewarded more handsomely than it had been with the Emperor. Another impressive piece of evidence for his own fineness of character and for his unerring judgment in singling out loyalty and devotion and steadfastness in others is afforded by the closing scene of his career. In the action in which he met his death, all his personal friends and messmates, with one exception, died fighting for his sake.[9]

---

[8] The only individual who went to this length was Orontas, and Orontas soon discovered that the monarch on whose loyalty he had relied was even less of a friend to the traitor than he was to Cyrus himself. [AUTHOR.]

[9] The exception was Ariaeus, who had been posted on the left in command of the cavalry and who fled with the whole force under his command as soon as he discovered that Cyrus had fallen. [AUTHOR.]

FIVE *CONDOTTIERI*

FIVE *CONDOTTIERI*

From Xenophon, *Cyrus' Expedition,* Book II, Chap. 6.

Five *Condottieri*

I must say something in appraisement of the generals whose arrest I have described, and who were subsequently sent up to the Emperor's court, where they met their death by decapitation.

Clearchus, the senior officer of the five, was universally acknowledged, by those who came into personal contact with him, to have been not only a born soldier but a passionate lover of war. So long as Lacedaemon remained at war with Athens, he did not go abroad; but as soon as peace was made he persuaded his government that the Thracians were misconducting themselves towards the Hellenes and, by hook or by crook, extracted permission from the Directory to undertake an overseas expedition against the Thracians in the hinterland of the Gallipoli Peninsula and of Perinthus.[1] The Directory for some reason repented of their decision when he was already beyond the frontiers, and attempted to stop him at the Isthmus of Corinth, but at that point he refused to obey orders and went off by sea to the Dardanelles — whereupon he was condemned to death, for disobeying orders, by the authorities at Sparta. As the exile that he

---

[1] The modern Eregli, on the north coast of the Sea of Marmara between Rodosto and San Stefano. [ED.]

now was, he presented himself to Cyrus. The arguments by which he prevailed upon the Prince have been recorded elsewhere, but the upshot was that Cyrus gave him ten thousand gold pieces. The receipt of this sum did not tempt Clearchus into leading a life of ease. Far from that, he employed the money for raising a force with which he made war upon the Thracians, and, after defeating this enemy in the field, he continued to raid their country and to protract his operations until the force was needed by Cyrus — whereupon he went off to fight on fresh fields by the Prince's side.

I think this record betrays a lover of war. When he might have enjoyed the blessings of peace without loss or dishonor, he chose to see service; when he might have led a life of ease, he preferred hard work if he could see service only on that condition; and, when he might have had money without danger, he chose by seeing service to diminish his funds. In fact, Clearchus longed to spend for war, much as ordinary people long to spend for pleasures, sensual or other. So much for his being a lover of war; and, as for his being a born soldier, that was evinced by the fact that he loved danger, never lost an opportunity by day or by night of leading an attack, and showed a cool head in crises, as was universally acknowledged by those who served with him on all his campaigns.

He also had the reputation of being a leader of men in so far as this was possible for a man of his character. He was as capable as any commander could be of taking

care that his troops were well supplied, and of getting
supplies together, and he showed no less capacity in impressing upon all around him that Clearchus was master.
This last result, however, was produced by harshness. He
had a scowling countenance, a rasping voice, and a way
of inflicting savage punishments — sometimes in anger —
with the consequence that on more than one occasion he
himself repented of his action. The punishments themselves, however, were a deliberate policy. In his view,
an army unchastened by punishment was worse than
useless; and there was current a saying of his to the
effect that a soldier ought to be more afraid of his commander than of the enemy if he was to be an efficient
sentry and was to keep his hands off his friends and was
to go into action without reasoning why. This meant that
in crises his troops were more than willing to obey him
and wanted no other leader. At such moments, it was
the saying that his scowl was transmuted into a smile
upon his men's faces, while his harshness formed an
impenetrable front against the enemy, until, to his own
side, it seemed harshness no longer but a saving grace.
On the other hand, when the crisis was surmounted and
the men were at liberty to go off and take service with
another commander, they repeatedly deserted Clearchus
in large numbers. The fact was that he had no charm
but was unvaryingly harsh and ferocious, so that the rela-
tion of his troops to their general was like that of school-
boys to their master. Certainly he never had troops who

followed him out of friendship or affection; but he maintained an exemplary discipline among whatever troops found themselves compulsorily under his orders — through being placed there by some government or through needing his leadership or through some other form of *force majeure*. It was when the troops began, under his leadership, to gain victories that their service-able qualities possessed the highest value; for, while their courage in the face of the enemy remained unimpaired, their fear of the chastisement meted out by Clearchus maintained their discipline.

While these were his characteristics as a leader, he did not enjoy the reputation of being a willing subordinate. When he met his death, he was about fifty years old.

Proxenus of Boeotia had cherished from his earliest childhood the ambition of fitting himself to be a great man of action, and in pursuance of this ambition he engaged the professional services of Gorgias of Leontini.[2] After studying under Gorgias, he felt himself fit at last to be a leader of men and to live on familiar terms with the great without being beholden to them; and he therefore embarked upon this enterprise with Cyrus, from which he hoped to win a great name, great power, and great sums of money. Although his ambitions were so

---

[2] A sophist or "uplifter," and one of the inventors of "rhetoric" — which might be translated as "viva-voce journalism." If Gorgias really lived to be 110 years old, he must probably be dated c. 470-360 B.C. [ED.]

extensive, it was nonetheless a transparent feature of his character that he would not care to satisfy any of these ambitions by immoral means. He felt that he must achieve his objects either consonantly with morality and honor or else not at all. He knew how to lead gentlemen, but he was not effective in impressing his troops with respect for, or awe of, his own personality. In fact, he was more sensitive to the opinion of his troops than his subordinates were to his opinion of them; and he allowed it to be obvious that he was more afraid of losing popularity with the troops than the troops were afraid of being insubordinate towards him. He believed that in order to be — and to be recognized as — a leader of men, it was sufficient to commend merit and to refrain from commending misconduct. For this reason, those of his comrades who were gentlemen cherished an affection for him, while bad characters used to intrigue against him because they thought him easy to manage. When he lost his life, he was about thirty years old.

Meno of Thessaly was undisguisedly ambitious of being immensely rich; ambitious of power, in order to make more money; and ambitious of honors, in order to realize higher profits still. He also desired to be friends with the great and mighty, in order that he might injure his fellows with impunity. For the accomplishment of his ambitions, he believed that the shortest cut was by way of perjury, untruthfulness, and duplicity, while straight-

forwardness and truthfulness were to his vision indistin-
guishable from feeble-mindedness. It was obviously that
he had no human feeling for anybody; and, whenever he
called himself somebody's friend, that was tantamount
to proof that he was intriguing against him. He never
depreciated an enemy and never spoke of any of his
comrades except in a depreciatory manner. He did not
scheme to get possession of enemy property, because he
considered that forewarned was forearmed; but he had
a secret which he fancied to be all his own and which
was that it was the easiest thing in the world to rob
friends off their guard. Whenever he detected a perjurer
or a bad character, he feared him as a man well armed,
whereas he did his best to take advantage of purity
and uprightness as being so many marks of unmanliness.
Just as ordinary people delight in truth and righteousness
and the fear of God, so Meno delighted in ability to de-
ceive, in the fabrication of falsehoods and in making
game of friends, while he invariably wrote off anyone
devoid of criminal instincts as deficient in education.
Whenever it was his object to hold the first place in anybody's affections, he conceived that the right way to gain
it was to slander those who held it already.

His contrivance for securing the obedience of his
troops was to make himself the accomplice of their misconduct. His claims to honor and consideration were
based upon a display of his extreme ability and extreme
readiness to injure his fellows. When anybody parted

company with him, he counted it a favor that he (Meno) had crossed his path without ruining him. Of course, in describing the inner man, there is always the possibility of misstatement at his expense, but the following stories are common knowledge. When he was still in his youthful bloom he extracted from Aristippus the command of the mercenaries; he became exceedingly intimate with an Oriental like Ariaeus through the possession of an unnatural taste in common; and he entered into relations with Tharypas, the unnaturalness of which was accentuated by the relative ages of the two men.

When Meno's colleagues were put to death because they had marched against the Emperor under Cyrus' banner, Meno himself, who had participated in their offense, did not share their punishment. The death penalty was not inflicted upon him by the Emperor until after the death of the others, and in his case it was not to be decapitation, which had been the fate of Clearchus and his companions and which is supposed to be almost instantaneous. Meno, less fortunate than they, is said to have been subjected to twelve months' lingering tortures before meeting the end of a malefactor.

Agias of Arcadia and Socrates of Achaïa both lost their lives with the rest. Neither of these officers was ever derided as a bad soldier or criticized as a poor friend. At the time of their death, they were each of them about five-and-thirty years of age.

CLEOMENES THE LAST OF SPARTA

CLEOMENES THE LAST OF SPARTA

c. 255-221 B.C.

From Plutarch, "Cleomenes," in *Parallel Lives* (Teubner text, ed. C. Sintenis, Vol. IV), Chap. 1; from Polybius, Book V, Chaps. 34-38; and from Plutarch, "Cleomenes," Chaps. 36-39.

Plutarch's principal source (besides Polybius, whom, in some passages, he reproduces almost word for word) was the historian Phylarchus of Naucratis (a Greek city-state in Egypt), who was Cleomenes' contemporary and admirer. Polybius drew largely upon the reminiscences (written and oral) of Aratus of Sicyon — the statesman who made the fortune of the Achaean Confederation and who successfully prevented Cleomenes from restoring the ancient ascendancy of Sparta over the other states in the Peloponnese. [Ed.]

Cleomenes the Last of Sparta

After the death of Agis,[1] his brother Archidamus at once fled the country before Leonidas [2] had succeeded in arresting him; but Agis' widow, with her infant child, was forcibly removed by Leonidas from her home in order to be joined in wedlock with his son Cleomenes. The boy was not really ripe for marriage, but his father was unwilling to see the lady given to any other husband, for Agiatis was heiress to the vast properties of her father Gylippus. She was also (in her bloom) by far the greatest beauty in Hellas, and she was sweet-natured as well. She is said to have struggled long and hard against the compulsion which was being put upon her; but, when once she had been mated with Cleomenes, she proved her character by reserving all her hatred for Leonidas and showing herself a good and loving wife to her youthful husband. From the moment when she had become his, the boy had fallen deeply in love with her, and he was able to sympathize, in a sense, with the feelings

---

[1] Agis IV of Sparta, who had been put to death (c. 240 B.C.) by his colleague Leonidas II for attempting to carry out a social revolution. [ED.]

[2] Agis' colleague on the throne and political opponent. [ED.]

cherished by his wife for Agis' memory. In fact, he used often to question her regarding Agis' story, and to listen with rapt attention to her reminiscences of her former husband's ideas and policy. Cleomenes possessed magnanimity and a lofty ambition, and he was a second Agis in his capacity for self-denial and simplicity of life; but he lacked the extraordinary scrupulousness and gentleness which had distinguished his predecessor. Passion was always ready to set spurs to his soul and to launch him in headlong pursuit of whatever object presented itself as praiseworthy at the moment. Cleomenes' ideal was to command willing allegiance, but he did not feel it wrong to impose his will upon others by violence for their own good.

❊   ❊   ❊

The Egyptian government had been accustomed (very properly) to pay great attention to foreign policy, but the new King [3] was negligent in his conduct of every department of public affairs owing to his scandalous *amours* and his senseless and continuous drinking. The natural consequence was that he very soon provoked a number of conspiracies against his throne and his life, the first of which was initiated by Cleomenes the Spartan.[4]

---

[3] Ptolemy IV Philopator, who came to the throne of Egypt in 222/1 B.C. [ED.]

[4] Cleomenes II had carried through by violence the social revolution at Sparta which Agis IV had failed to carry through by constitutional methods; but the forcible cancellation of debts and redistribution of land, by which he had restored Sparta's military

The sovereign with whom Cleomenes had formed personal ties and had entered into political co-operation had been Ptolemy "The Benefactor," and, so long as this ruler remained alive, the exile had possessed his soul in patience, in the constant assurance of obtaining from his ally the necessary assistance for the recovery of his ancestral throne. After "The Benefactor's" death, however, the time passed, while the situation in Hellas was calling aloud for Cleomenes' intervention. Antigonus was dead; the Achaeans were beset by enemies; and, in her feud against Achaïa and Macedonia, Lacedaemon had found a partner in the shape of Aetolia — the very combination originally projected by Cleomenes himself. All this forced Cleomenes into making more strenuous efforts than ever to get away from Alexandria. He began by petitioning the government to send him overseas with the necessary troops and supplies; but, when he found his representations ignored, he narrowed down his demands to an urgent request for the issue of passports to himself alone and his personal household. The mere situation, he

---

man power, had alarmed the upper and middle classes in the other Peloponnesian states, who felt themselves threatened in their private property as well as in their political independence. The opposition to Cleomenes had rallied round Aratus of Sicyon, the leading statesman of the Achaean Confederation, and Aratus had purchased the intervention of Antigonus Doson, the Regent of Macedon, by surrendering to him the citadel of Corinth. In 222/1 the united Achaean and Macedonian forces had defeated the Lacedaemonians at Sellasia. Sparta itself had been occupied, and Cleomenes had barely succeeded in escaping overseas to become a refugee at the court of Alexandria. [ED.]

argued, offered him sufficient facilities for securing his
ancestral dominions.

The King, for the reasons which I have mentioned,
gave no attention to public questions and no forethought
to the future, and he showed his senseless imbecility in
the present case by the consistency with which he ignored Cleomenes. Sosibius, on the other hand, who was
prime minister at the time, held a council on the subject
with his colleagues, which resulted in substantially the
following decisions being taken in regard to Cleomenes.
They did not favor the idea of sending Cleomenes overseas with naval support and supplies, because the death
of Antigonus had made their minds easy in regard to the
foreign situation and they felt that the expense involved
would be incurred for nothing. In addition, they were
in mortal terror — now that Antigonus was dead and no
other statesman was left in Hellas of Cleomenes' caliber
— lest the exile might make himself master of Hellas in
a moment, without a struggle, and might then prove, in
his turn, a serious and formidable opponent of Egypt.
After all, he had surveyed her condition with his own
eyes; he had learned to take her King at his true worth;
and he had his eye upon all those straggling and distant
enclaves of the Egyptian dominions which offered so
many ways and means to an enterprising statesman.
There was a considerable naval squadron, for instance,
at Samos and a large body of troops at Ephesus.

For the above-mentioned reasons they rejected Cleo-

menes' project in so far as it involved sending him overseas with supplies; while, on the other hand, they felt it
altogether incompatible with Egyptian interests so completely to discount the potentialities of such a man as to
let him leave Egypt as her manifest and embittered
enemy. The alternative was to detain him in Egypt
against his will. That, however, was unanimously rejected out of hand, and without discussion. It was felt
to be too hazardous an experiment for the lamb and the
lion to lie down together; and this was the point which
aroused the greatest anxiety in Sosibius' own mind. . . .

Sosibius made every effort to arouse the King and his
court to take the offensive and to place Cleomenes under
lock and key; and, in working for the realization of this
plan, he availed himself of the following assistance.
There was a certain Nicagoras of Messene who had been
a family friend of Archidamus, King of Lacedaemon.[5]
Until the time when Archidamus fled from Sparta for
fear of Cleomenes [6] and appeared in Messenia, the two
men had had little to do with one another; but from then
onwards, when Nicagoras had welcomed Archidamus
to his house and had hospitably supplied his wants, they
were constantly together, until they became whole-
hearted and familiar friends. Accordingly, when, at a
later date, Cleomenes held out to Archidamus hopes of

---

[5] Archidamus was the brother of Agis IV, who had slipped
through the hands of Cleomenes' father, Leonidas, after Agis had
been judicially murdered. [ED.]

[6] More accurately, for fear of Leonidas. [ED.]

return and reconciliation, Nicagoras took charge of the
negotiations and the exchange of guarantees. Upon the
ratification of these, Archidamus proceeded to return to
Sparta, in reliance upon the terms which Nicagoras had
obtained for him, whereupon Cleomenes came to meet
him and took his life, though he spared Nicagoras and
his victim's other companions. To outsiders, Nicagoras
simulated gratitude toward Cleomenes for his salvation,
but inwardly he had taken the tragedy to heart, in the
feeling that he had been responsible for leading King
Archidamus to his destruction.

A short time before the cabinet council, Nicagoras had
arrived in harbor at Alexandria with a cargo of remounts;
and, in disembarking from his ship, he had encountered
Cleomenes and Panteus, as well as Hippitas, strolling
along the quays. When Cleomenes saw him, he went up
to him, greeted him warmly, and asked him what brought
him to Egypt. Upon Nicagoras' explaining that he had
come with a cargo of remounts, Cleomenes remarked
that he was only sorry that Nicagoras had not come, instead, with a cargo of *cocottes* and *catamites,* for those
were the goods which the present King was after. At
the moment, Nicagoras merely laughed and said nothing;
but, a few days later, when he had been brought into
close relations with Sosibius on business connected with
the remounts, he repeated against Cleomenes the remark
just recorded, and, when he saw Sosibius prick up his
ears, he detailed to him the whole story of his old

feud with the Spartan King. Realizing the Messenian's hostility toward Cleomenes, Sosibius paid him down money on the spot, and promised him more later, as an inducement to write a letter against Cleomenes, which he was to leave behind under his seal — the intention being that, at an interval of a few days after Nicagoras had sailed again from Alexandria, a servant should present the letter to Sosibius with the statement that it had been sent by Nicagoras himself.

Nicagoras lent his assistance to the scheme; the letter was brought to Sosibius by the servant after Nicagoras' departure; and the prime minister promptly took servant and letter along with him to the King. The servant declared that Nicagoras had left the letter behind with instructions to deliver it to Sosibius, and the letter itself enlarged upon Cleomenes' intention of revolting against His Majesty's Government unless they sent him on his expedition overseas with the proper armaments and supplies. Sosibius promptly seized upon this handle and urged the King and the rest of the court to lose no time in securing themselves against Cleomenes by placing him under lock and key. This was now actually done, a palatial mansion being assigned to the prisoner, in which he was to reside under surveillance. However, his position differed from that of other prisoners merely in the fact that he had a roomier place of confinement at his disposal.

Realizing this position, and filled with pessimism in

regard to the future, Cleomenes decided to resort to extremes. He was influenced not so much by any conviction that his project could succeed — there was, indeed, no rational justification for it — as by his eagerness to die a noble death before being forced to submit to indignities unworthy of his gallant antecedents. It is also my belief that his mind was not insensible to an ideal which is apt to present itself to magnanimous natures:

"If die I must, by Fate's unswerving aim,

I will not listless die, nor without fame,

But in the doing of some mighty deed

By which those after me shall know my name." [7]

*   *   *

There was a member of the Egyptian court named Ptolemy, son of Chrysermus, who had always been polite to Cleomenes, so that they were on terms of some familiarity and intimacy. Cleomenes now asked Ptolemy to visit him in prison, and Ptolemy not only came but talked with him gently, with the object of removing his suspicions and making out the best case possible for the King. As he was leaving the house to go home, Cleomenes followed at his heels, without his noticing it, to attend him to the door; and there on the doorstep Ptolemy severely reprimanded the sentries for "being so criminally careless in guarding a great wild beast like that, which it was hard enough anyway to keep under control." After hearing these words with his own ears,

---

[7] *Iliad*, Book XXII, lines 303-305. [ED.]

Cleomenes slipped away before Ptolemy became aware of his presence and repeated them to his friends. The whole party at once abandoned the hopes which till that moment they had been cherishing and determined, in their anger, to take vengeance upon King Ptolemy for the wrong which they had suffered at his insolent hands and in so doing to win a death worthy of Sparta instead of waiting to be fattened like victims for the slaughter. It was intolerable to their minds that Cleomenes, who had been too proud to come to terms with a gallant soldier and man of action like Antigonus, should sit awaiting the convenience of a royal dancing-dervish who was going to put him to death the next time that he laid aside his tambourine and paused in his celebrations.

After they had formed this resolution, chance gave them their opportunity by sending King Ptolemy on a flying visit to Canopus. First of all, they spread the rumor that Cleomenes was being released from prison by the King's orders; and then Cleomenes' friends took advantage of a royal tradition by which presents and dishes were always sent on the King's behalf to persons about to be released from custody, in order to procure provisions of this kind from outside in large quantities and send them in to Cleomenes. The sentries were beguiled into the belief that their royal master was the donor; and Cleomenes slaughtered one beast after another as sacrificial offerings and lavished the perquisites upon the guards, while he decorated his friends with garlands and settled down to banquet in their company. He is said, however, to have plunged into action at an earlier moment than he had intended, after becoming aware that one of his servants, who was privy to his plans, had been spending the night out at the house of a sweetheart. Fearing denunciation, and seeing that it was now noon and that the sentries were dead-drunk already, Cleomenes put on his shirt, unstitched the seam above the right shoulder,[8] and sprang out into the street with drawn sword and with twelve [9] friends, in the same guise, to back him.

Hippitas, though lame, tumbled out gamely enough with the rest at the first spurt, but he soon saw that his companions were slackening their pace on his account, whereat he besought them to run him through and not to wreck the enterprise by waiting behind for a useless fellow like himself. At that moment, a native of Alexandria came leading a horse past the gate; so they took the animal away from its owner, put up Hippitas into the saddle, and then swept at the double through the streets, calling upon the people to rise for liberty. The good people of Alexandria appear to have possessed just sufficient spirit to inspire them with admiration for Cleomenes' audacity, but not a soul ventured to follow and lend a hand. Ptolemy, son of Chrysermus, met his death

---

[8] In order to leave his sword arm free. [ED.]

[9] The word "thirteen," in the original Greek, seems intended, by the order and construction of the words, to include Cleomenes himself. [ED.]

at the hands of three members of the band, who fell upon him just as he was coming out of the palace. Another Ptolemy, who was responsible for the security of the city, bore down upon them in a carriage, whereupon the party charged him, dispersed his escort and attendants, pulled the functionary himself out of the carriage, and killed him likewise. After that, they made for the citadel, with the intention of breaking open the prison and utilizing the man power of its inmates. The sentries, however, barricaded themselves securely before the assailants arrived. After being foiled in this final stroke, Cleomenes went on wandering at random through the city, while not a soul joined but everybody ran away in consternation.

At last he gave it up, remarking to his friends that after all it was no wonder if men who ran away from liberty were ruled by women, and then he adjured them all to die a death that would do honor to himself and to their achievements. The example was given by Hippitas, who received his deathblow from one of the younger men of whom he asked the favor. Thereafter, each of the party calmly and fearlessly took his own life, except for Panteus, who had been the first over the wall at the capture of Megalopolis. Panteus, the handsomest and most athletic young Spartan of his generation, had been a favorite of the King's, and Cleomenes had ordered him to defer his own death until he saw that Cleomenes himself and all his companions had fallen. When all lay prone, Panteus went round from one to another and grazed each with his dagger in order to test whether any of them were still alive after all. Upon pricking Cleomenes close to the ankle, he saw his features contract; so he kissed him and then sat down beside him. At last, when all was over, he embraced the corpse and slew himself upon it.

Cleomenes had been King of Sparta for sixteen heroic years [10] when he met his end in this fashion. After the news had spread from end to end of the city, Cratesiclea,[11] noble woman though she was, lost her self-command under the shock of the calamity and wailed aloud as she clasped Cleomenes' children in her arms. The elder of the two children darted away and threw himself headlong from the roof — a reaction which, in a child, could have been expected by nobody. He was seriously but not fatally injured, and was picked up screaming in protest at being prevented from putting an end to himself. As soon as King Ptolemy heard the story, he ordered Cleomenes' corpse to be first flayed and then crucified, and the children and their grandmother and her ladies-in-waiting to be put to death.

Among the latter was the wife of Panteus — a woman of very great beauty and very great nobility of feature. She and Panteus were newly married and in the full flower of their love when their fates overtook them. The

---

10 C. 236-221 B.C. [ED.]
11 Cleomenes' mother. His wife Agiatis had died at Sparta just before the Battle of Sellasia. [ED.]

lady herself had wished to accompany Panteus overseas [12] at the beginning, but had been prevented by her
parents, who had placed her forcibly under lock and
key and had kept her under surveillance. It was not long,
however, before she secured a horse and a little money,
escaped under cover of night, galloped without slackening rein to Taenarum,[13] and there embarked on board a
ship bound for Egypt. She safely reached her husband,
and thenceforth shared his life of exile with cheerfulness
and even with gaiety. This lady now gave her arm to
Cratesiclea as she was being marched away by the soldiers. She held up her mantle for her and breathed encouragement into her ear — though Cratesiclea herself
was not in the least appalled at the prospect of death,
but had only one prayer, which was that she might be
allowed to die before the children. When they arrived
at the place where the executioners ordinarily did their
work, they started by slaughtering the children before
Cratesiclea's eyes, and only then addressed themselves
to Cratesiclea herself. Her immeasurable tragedy drew
from her the one cry: "Children, children, whither have
you gone?"

Panteus' wife, who was tall and strong, girt up her skirt
and began — quietly and without a word — to attend to
each of the dying women and to shroud their bodies as

---

[12] Only a small band of Spartans, of whom Panteus had been
one, had accompanied Cleomenes into exile after the disaster at
Sellasia. [ED.]

[13] Porto Quaglio, at the southern tip of the Mani Peninsula. [ED.]

well as circumstances allowed. Last of all, she composed her own dress, drew her shawl down around her, permitted no one to approach or to be a witness except the actual executioner, and then died a heroic death, without requiring any hand to compose her dress for her or to draw it round her after her ordeal was over. Her spirit did not lose its composure even in death, but preserved for her body the screen in which she had enveloped it before she ceased to breathe.

Thus Lacedaemon, in her last appearance upon the stage of history, cast her women for a second tragedy, to dispute the palm with the tragedy of her men [14] — demonstrating thereby that her nobility was invulnerable to the insults of outrageous fortune.

A few days afterwards, the sentries on guard over the body of Cleomenes, where it hung upon the cross, saw a huge snake coiled round the head and covering the face, so that no carrion bird alighted on it. At this, the terrors of religion assailed the King and set his womenfolk to work upon a fresh round of ritual — in atonement for the death of a man who was manifestly beloved of God and of more than mortal nature. As for the people of Alexandria, they made the spot a place of pilgrimage and entitled Cleomenes a saint and a son of God.

---

[14] In the Hellenic world, plays were usually produced in batches at dramatic festivals in which the authors competed for a prize. [ED.]

CATO THE ELDER

CATO THE ELDER

(Marcus Porcius Cato)

c. 234-149 B.C.

From Plutarch, "Cato Major," in *Parallel Lives* (Teubner text, ed. C. Sintenis, Vol. II), Chaps. 1, 2-3, 4, 20-24.

Cato the Elder

Marcus Cato's family is said to have come originally from Tusculum, though Cato lived and worked on an ancestral farm in the Sabina before he entered upon his military and political career. While his ancestors appear to have been quite obscure, Cato himself praises his father Marcus as a good soldier and a fine character and records that his great-grandfather was frequently decorated for valor.[1] The colloquial expression at Rome for people of undistinguished birth who are beginning to make a name for themselves on their own merits is "New Men," and this expression was applied, in his time, to Cato — a circumstance which drew from this "New Man" the remark that he was new enough to office and honors but as old as the hills in ancestral qualities and achievements. . . .

In the neighborhood of Cato's farm was the cottage that had once belonged to Manius Curius,[2] and to this shrine Cato was a frequent pilgrim. The impression

---

[1] He adds the details that he lost five chargers on the field of battle and was five times reimbursed by the Treasury as a tribute to his gallantry. [AUTHOR.]

[2] The hero of the three triumphs. [AUTHOR.]

made upon his eye by the diminutiveness of the allot-
ment and the simplicity of the dwelling house branded
itself in his imagination into an impression of the character of the hero who rose to be the greatest man at Rome,
imposed her yoke upon the most warlike nations in the
world, and drove Pyrrhus out of Italy — yet who did not
cease, after three triumphs, to cultivate this tiny allot-
ment with his own hands and to live in this cottage. It
was here that the Samnite mission found him sitting by
the hearth and boiling turnips when they offered him an
immense bribe — whereupon Curius dismissed them
with the remark that for a man who could dine on turnips
money was superfluous and that, for his own satisfaction,
he did not care to possess money so much as to conquer
its possessors. Cato used to go home with his mind full
of the legend; and, when he once more surveyed his own
house, farm, slaves, and fare, he would exact from himself a still higher standard of work on the land and a still
lower standard of luxury.

When Fabius Maximus captured the city of Tarentum,[3]
Cato happened to be serving under his command as quite
a lad, and at this time he formed a friendship with a
member of the Pythagorean school of philosophy named
Nearchus, whose principles aroused his curiosity. His
friend gave him an exposition of the same arguments
that Plato uses when he stigmatizes Pleasure as a deadly
temptation and the Body as the original misfortune of

---
[3] In 209 B.C. [ED.]

the Soul, and finds the Soul's release and purification in
the principles which best enable her to disentangle and
disengage herself from bodily affections; and this instruc-
tion confirmed Cato in his love of simplicity and self-
denial. In other spheres, however, he is said to have been
an eleventh-hour disciple of Hellenic culture. Apparently it was not until an extremely advanced age that
he took up Hellenic literature, when he profited a little
from Thucydides and rather more from Demosthenes in
the art of public speaking. On the other hand, his works
are reasonably well embroidered with Hellenic senti-
ments and anecdotes, while many passages translated
word for word from the Greek are included in his apoph-
thegms and aphorisms.

An important part in Cato's career was played by
Valerius Flaccus, a gentleman who belonged to one of
the most distinguished families in Rome, who possessed
influence, and who not only was acute in detecting
promise in others but showed a disinterested kindness in
assisting it, by encouragement, to achieve recognition.
Flaccus, whose estates adjoined Cato's farm, heard
stories from his servants of Cato's frugal living and of
his working with his own hands; he was amazed at their
description of how, the first thing in the morning, Cato
would go to the *piazza* and give his services to suitors in
court, and how he would then go home to his farm and,
after changing into a vest (in wintertime) or stripping
to the skin (in the summer), would labor in the fields

with his servants until he closed the day's work by sup-
ping off the same bread and wine as they and at the same
table. Flaccus' servants had so much to tell of Cato's
good feeling and good sense, with one or two epigram-
matic sayings of his coinage, that finally Flaccus gave
orders that Cato should be asked to dinner. From that
day onwards he sought his society and, discerning in him
a tractable and refined character in need of cultivation,
light, and air, he prevailed upon him to enter the field of
Roman politics. . . .

Cato records of himself that he never in his life wore
clothes costing more than one hundred drachmas; that
as praetor and consul he drank the same wine as the
common laborer; that he seasoned his bread for supper
with thirty coppers' worth of snacks from the market,
and that this he did out of patriotism in order to keep
himself physically fit for active service. He adds that
when, as the result of a legacy, he found himself the
possessor of an Oriental embroidered rug, he sold it immediately; that none of his farm buildings was white-
washed; and that he never bought a slave for more than
1500 drachmas, being a master who had no use for delicate slaves with handsome faces but who wanted hard
workers of sturdy builds like grooms and herdsmen —
while even in their case, when they reached old age, he
made it his principle to sell them off, in order not to have
idle mouths to feed. He laid down the law that nothing

was cheap which was superfluous and that an unneces-
sary object bought for a copper was bought too dear.
As he put it himself, "seedlings and fatlings are better
bargains than sprinklings and sweepings." [4] . . .

He showed himself a good father and husband and a
redoubtable man of business who never treated the management of his affairs as a trivial or sordid occupation of
secondary importance; and I therefore propose to describe what redounds to his credit in these relationships.
He married a wife whose birth was superior to her fortune, with the idea that, although in the matter of pride
and haughtiness there was nothing to choose between
heiresses and aristocrats, the latter were more amenable
to their husbands on points of honor owing to their hor-
ror of unladylike behavior. Wife-beating and child-beat-
ing were described by Cato as laying violent hands on
the holiest of holies. He pronounced it a greater glory
to be a good husband than to be a great senator, and
he supported this by remarking that the only characteristic which he admired in Socrates — the philosopher of
an earlier age — was his unfailing goodness and gentleness in his relations with an ill-tempered wife and a family of afflicted children.

After the birth of Cato's boy, no business except
certain public duties was so urgent as to hinder the father

---

[4] I.e., agricultural produce and livestock are better bargains than
perfumes and spices. [ED.]

from being on the spot when the mother was bathing the baby and swaddling it. Cato's wife was her own wet nurse, and she would frequently offer her breast to her slaves' infants as well, in order to secure a place in their hearts for her son as the foster brother of their children. When the boy arrived at the dawn of understanding, Cato took his education in hand himself, although he possessed an accomplished slave-tutor named Chilon, who had a number of boys under his professional charge. However, as Cato himself explains, he did not choose to be beholden to a slave for imparting knowledge of such importance; so the father combined in his own person the duties of tutor, instructor in law, and trainer in athletics, in which capacity he taught his son not only to throw the javelin, to fight in harness, and to ride, but also to box, to endure heat and cold, and to force his way swimming through the worst swirls and eddies of the river. He likewise mentions that he composed his histories in his own handwriting and in bold characters, in order that the boy might profit by a store of knowledge regarding the national past within the four walls of his home. He tells us, further, that he was as careful to avoid obscene language in the presence of his son as in that of the holy Vestal Virgins, and that he never took a bath in his company.[5] Bent as Cato thus was upon

---

[5] This appears to have been a general social convention at Rome. Sons-in-law, for instance, were careful not to take a bath in the company of their fathers-in-law, because modesty forbade them

forming and fashioning his son into a model of excellence, he discovered that — while there was no fault to find with the boy's endeavor and while his spirit displayed the willingness of a noble breed — his physical constitution was apparently too delicate for hard labor, whereupon the father relaxed for his benefit the over-severe and strenuous features in his regime.

In spite of his physique, young Cato distinguished himself on active service, and fought brilliantly under Paullus' command in the battle against Perseus.[6] In the course of the battle his sword either was struck from his grasp by a blow or else slipped out of his moist hand— a *contretemps* which so much distressed him that he addressed himself to some of his comrades and flung himself at their head upon the enemy once again. After a long and violent struggle, he cleared the place where the accident had occurred and with much difficulty discovered the sword buried under piles of arms and heaps of corpses, in which the Roman and enemy dead were indiscriminately mingled. This exploit won for the lad the admiration of no less a person than the commander-in-chief, while a letter addressed to his son by Cato himself is also mentioned in which the father loaded him with praises for the keenness and sense of honor which

---

to uncover their nakedness. On the other hand, when they afterwards acquired from the Hellenes the habit of stripping naked they retorted by infecting the latter with the less desirable practice of doing the same thing in mixed company. [AUTHOR.]

[6] The Battle of Pydna (168 B.C.) [ED.]

he had displayed in the incident of the sword. Afterwards the young man maintained his connection with Paullus by marrying his daughter Tertia, the sister of Scipio Aemilianus — the honor of allying himself with a family of such eminence being by that time conferred upon him in his own right as much as for his father's sake. The pains spent by Cato upon his son were thus well rewarded.

Cato used to acquire large numbers of slaves, his favorite purchases being child-prisoners still young enough to be bred and trained like pups or colts. None of these slaves ever set foot in a strange house without being sent expressly by Cato himself or by Cato's wife. If asked how Cato was, the messenger would answer simply: "I don't know." At home any slave of Cato's was required to be either at work or asleep. Cato highly approved of long sleepers, believing that they were more good-natured than wakeful souls and that in every occasion of life there was better service to be had from people who enjoyed their sleep than from people in want of sleep. In the belief that sexual appetite was at the root of the worst criminality among slaves, he arranged that his slaves might have intercourse with the maids on payment of a money fee, while prohibiting all connection with any other women. At the beginning of his career, when he was still a poor man and was engaged on active service, he was never put out by hardships of diet and used to denounce it as a disgrace that anyone should squabble with a slave for the sake of the belly. Afterwards, when his affairs began to prosper, he took to giving dinner parties for friends and official colleagues, on which occasions he used to chastise slovenly waiting or bad service — giving the culprit a taste of the strap the instant after the guests had risen from table. He invariably contrived that his slaves should have some bone of contention to keep them at odds with one another, and the portent of harmony among them aroused his fear and suspicion. When any slaves were held to have committed capital offenses, it was his principle to bring them for trial before a court of the whole household and to inflict the death penalty if the verdict went against them.

As he began to address himself more strenuously to profit-making, he came to look upon agriculture as a recreation rather than a source of income and made it his policy to invest in safe and solid concerns by acquiring lakes, mineral springs, sites devoted to the fulling trade, or remunerative land containing natural pasturage and timber, which brought him in high dividends and which — to use Cato's own words — were immune from injury even by Zeus himself. He also speculated in marine ventures, which have a worse name than any other form of speculation but in which he safeguarded himself in the following way: He used to require the borrowers to form a company with a large number of shareholders; and then, if fifty shareholders and as many ships were forthcoming, he used himself to hold a single share in the name of a freedman called Quinctio, who was in partnership with the borrowers and who sailed as supercargo. This meant that the risk was very widely distributed, while the profits to be gained were enormous. Cato would also advance funds to any of his slaves who asked for them, and with these funds the slaves used to purchase boys in order to resell them at the end of a year after training and instructing them at Cato's expense. Many of these boys were actually retained by Cato himself, who would credit the trainer with the highest price offered for them in the market. In exhorting his son to be a good businessman, Cato remarks that to diminish assets is permissible for widows and not for men. Our hero really goes too far, however, when he ventures to eulogize as an inspired genius the man who leaves on the credit side of his ledger more than twice as much as he originally found there.

Cato was quite an old man when an Athenian mission headed by the two philosophers, Carneades of the Academy and Diogenes of the Stoa, appeared at Rome [7] in order to appeal against a judgment that had been given against the Athenian government.[8] At once the leading literary lights among the younger generation flocked around the visitors and sat at their feet, where they lis-

---

[7] In 156 B.C. [ED.]

[8] The Oropian government had been the plaintiff, and the Megarian government the arbitrator by whom Athens had been condemned; the Athenian case had gone by default; and the reparations had been assessed at 500 talents. [AUTHOR.] Moreover, Athens had been flagrantly in the wrong. [ED.]

tened with admiration to their words of wisdom. Carneades' charm exercised a particularly strong fascination and won a fully proportionate reputation; and, when it secured crowded and enthusiastic audiences, it filled the city with the sound of a mighty rushing wind. The tale spread of how a Hellene — consummate in the art of dazzling the imagination and irresistible as a "spellbinder" — had inspired the younger generation with a burning passion which had driven them from the path of all other pleasures and pursuits and had transformed them into enthusiasts for philosophy. This movement found favor with most people at Rome, who were delighted to see the children imbibing Hellenic culture and sitting at the feet of such highly admired personalities.

Cato, however, had been annoyed from the very beginning to think that this literary mania should be stealing a march upon the country, because he was afraid that the young men might turn their ambitions in this direction and might prefer to make their reputations as speakers rather than as soldiers and men of action. Accordingly when the philosophers' reputation increased in the country by leaps and bounds, and their first speech before the Senate was interpreted for them by so prominent a person as Gaius Aquillius — who had set his heart upon this role and had begged it of them as a favor — Cato decided to find some diplomatic way of exorcising all the philosophers from the country. With this object he rose in the Senate and criticized the government on the ground that a foreign mission had been waiting for months in Rome without having succeeded in transacting its business, notwithstanding the fact that its members were gentlemen who could convince you in a moment upon any point they pleased. He submitted that the Senate should lose no time in taking a decision and passing a resolution in the matter of this mission, in order that its distinguished members might return to their academic occupations and might discourse to the children of Hellas, while young men at Rome attended to the laws and to the authorities as they had always done before.

Cato did not take this step because he objected to Carneades, as is sometimes supposed, but because he had a quarrel with philosophy in general and was misguided by intolerance into vituperating the whole of culture and art. His account of Socrates, for example, is that he was a loquacious and violent personage who attempted, as far as in him lay, to make himself master in his country by destroying morality and by artificially distorting his neighbors' opinions into contradiction with the law. He pours ridicule upon Socrates' course of studies by remarking that his pupils grew old at his feet, as though they were going to practice their profession and to plead cases before Minos' court in the Kingdom of Hades. Finally, he attempts to prejudice his son against Hellenic civilization by a dictum which sounds somewhat audacious on the lips of age. He solemnly prophesizes that, if Rome saturates herself with Hellenic literature, she will lose her Empire. However, the emptiness of this dismal foreboding has been exposed by time, in the course of which Rome has risen to the pinnacle of her imperial greatness while opening her arms to Hellenic studies and Hellenic culture in every form.

Not content with waging war upon Hellenic philosophers, Cato kept a suspicious eye upon the Hellenic physicians practicing at Rome. His attention appears to have been drawn to an observation made by Hippocrates when the Persian Emperor offered him some vast number of talents if he would come to court — an offer to which the sage retorted with the remark that he would never place his services at the disposal of non-Hellenic enemies of Hellas. This, Cato used to say, was the creed of the entire medical profession,[9] and he used to exhort his boy to beware of the whole tribe. In this connection he mentions a treatise of his own composition, which he used as a guide for nursing and dieting invalids at home. Apparently he never kept any patient upon a starvation diet, but fed them on vegetables or on tender meat like duck, pigeon, or hare. This diet, he maintained, was sufficiently light to be suitable for invalids, the only drawback being that it induces in patients a plethora of dreams. This particular regime of nursing and diet, so he asserts, has not only suited his own health but has

[9] The assumption being that every doctor was a Hellene. [ED.]

enabled him to preserve the health of his family. On the latter point, he can hardly claim to have escaped the wrath to come, for he had the misfortune to lose both his wife and his son. On the other hand, his own physical constitution was so impregnably fit and strong that he was marvelously well preserved — so much so that he was capable of sexual relations in extreme old age and actually contracted a marriage altogether out of keeping with his years.

This marriage had a history, which begins with the loss of his first wife. After that bereavement, Cato found a wife for his son in the person of Paullus' daughter, the sister of Scipio, while he consoled his own widowerhood by a *liaison* with a maid who used to pay him private visits. In a cramped house, and that with a bride in it, there was no concealing the scandal; and on one occasion, when the young woman bustled perhaps rather too brazenly past the room, the bridegroom, though he uttered not a word, gave her a somewhat sour look and betrayed his agitation in a manner that did not escape the old gentleman's eye. Realizing that the situation was becoming objectionable to the young couple, Cato made no complaints or reproaches but, in going down to the *piazza*, as he always did, with an escort of friends, he accosted one of his former second-division clerks named Salonius, who was among the party attending him on the present occasion, and asked him in an exceedingly loud voice whether he had yet betrothed his little daughter to anybody. The good man replied that he would never even think of doing such a thing without first consulting Cato.

"Well," Cato continued, "I have found you a very suitable son-in-law — unless, by the way, there might be objections on the score of age. Otherwise there is no fault to be found with him, but he is an extremely old man."

Salonius began to beg his patron to take charge of the business and to betroth the girl to the man of his choice, considering that she was Cato's *protégée* and was dependent on his good offices — whereat Cato made no more ado but broke it to him that he was suitor in his own behalf. At the first blush, not unnaturally, this announcement reduced the good man to stupefaction — imagining, as he had done, that Cato was worlds removed from marriage, as far removed, in fact, as Salonius was himself from matrimonial alliances with consular families and with the heroes of triumphs. When he saw, however, that Cato was in earnest, he accepted thankfully; so they went straight down to the *piazza* and proceeded to execute the deed of betrothal. These preparations for marriage caused Cato's son to come with his friends in a body and to ask his father whether the proposed introduction of a mother-in-law into the household was a reflection upon his own filial conduct.

Cato's reply was to roar out: "Not a word! My dear boy, not a word! Your behavior towards me is irreproachable and I have not a single fault to find. I am only anxious to leave behind me more sons of mine and more citizens for the country of the same stamp as you."

SCIPIO THE YOUNGER

SCIPIO THE YOUNGER

(Publius Cornelius Scipio Aemilianus)

c. 185-129 B.C.

Translated from Polybius, Book XXXI, Chaps. 23-25,
29-30.

Scipio the Younger

Now that the progress of my narrative, and the period to which it has brought me, have concentrated my attention upon the house of Lucius Aemilius Paullus, I propose to satisfy my readers' curiosity by fulfilling a promise which has been left undischarged in the preceding volume. I promised there to explain why and how it was that Scipio's [1] reputation in Rome soared upwards with such abnormal and dazzling rapidity, and incidentally how it was the Polybius' friendship and intimacy with Scipio grew to such a degree that its fame spread not only to the bounds of Italy and Hellas but to the remoter parts of the world, where their mutual attraction and constant companionship became an equally familiar story. The origin of the relationship between these two men, which arose out of the reading and discussion of certain literary works, has been described already. Their intimacy was increasing at the time when the hostages [2] were being banished from Rome to the Confederate

---

[1] Publius Cornelius Scipio Aemilianus Africanus Minor, son of Lucius Aemilius Paullus, grandson by adoption of Publius Cornelius Scipio Africanus Major. [ED.]

[2] After the third Romano-Macedonian war had ended in the victory of Rome, the Roman government summoned to Italy over a thousand notables from Achaïa, Boeotia, Aetolia, Acarnania, and

85

States in Italy; and on this occasion Lucius' boys Fabius
and Scipio pleaded with the praetor [3] that Polybius
might be permitted to remain in Rome. After the grant-
ing of this petition, the companionship of the friends
made rapid strides until it culminated in the following
incident:

When the whole party were leaving Fabius' house together one day, it happened that Fabius turned off
towards the *piazza* while Polybius went in the opposite
direction with Scipio. As they walked, Publius — speaking in a low and gentle voice and blushing as he spoke
— addressed Polybius with the following appeal: "Polybius, I have something to ask you. Here are we two
brothers eating at the same board. Why is it that you
talk all the time to Fabius and address all your questions
and observations to him, while you pass me over? Evi-
dently, I am afraid, you too hold the same opinion of me
as is held apparently by my fellow countrymen. Everybody, so I hear, regards me as a quiet, unenterprising
fellow, worlds removed from the normal Roman career
and the normal Roman activities — and all because I do
not choose to practice at the bar. This, people say, is not
at all the kind of representative that is wanted by the

Epirus (though all these states had remained neutral during the
war), and then detained them in Italy for seventeen or eighteen
years, the survivors not being liberated until the eyar 151/0 B.C.
Polybius himself was one of the hostages from Achaïa. [ED.]

[3] The officer within whose department the disposal of the hostages fell. [ED.]

house of which I am a member — in fact, just the contrary; and that is what wounds me most of all."

Polybius was taken aback by such an overture from a lad who was at that time not more than eighteen years old, but he replied as follows: "I beg and entreat you, my dear Scipio, not to speak of such a thing and not even to think of it for a moment. I am not looking down upon you or passing you over when I do what you describe — far from it! It is simply because your brother is older than you that I turn to him at the beginning and again at the end of our conversations and that I direct to him my observations and advice — my assumption being that you share his opinions. Moreover, I am surprised to hear from you now that you feel it wounding to be regarded as gentler than members of your house are expected to be, for it is as clear as day that you are really proud of the imputation. Personally, I should be delighted to place my own services at your disposal and to assist you to do credit to your ancestors as a speaker and a man of action. As regards the studies upon which I observe that you and your brother are concentrating your efforts and ambitions for the time being, you will not find any lack of eager assistants for both of you. A whole tribe of these gentlemen is pouring into Rome from Hellas here and now under our eyes. In regard, however, to the points which are wounding you (as you tell me) particularly deeply at the moment, I believe that you could find no better ally and assistant than myself."

Before Polybius had finished speaking, the young man seized his right hand in both his own and squeezed it impulsively, with the words: "If only I might see the day on which you put everything else aside in order to attend to *me* and to share my life with me! From that moment onwards I shall feel myself a credit to my house and to my ancestors."

This interview left Polybius a prey to mingled feelings of pleasure and perplexity — pleasure at seeing the lad's eagerness and receptivity, and perplexity at realizing the eminence of the family and the affluence of its members. However, after this mutual covenant, the lad would never be parted from Polybius and put everything else aside in order to enjoy his company. From that time onwards without intermission, the two friends gave one another practical proof of their devotion in the trials of daily life, until their mutual attraction and affection for one another became as close as the family tie between father and son.

The first goal towards which Scipio's high impulse and endeavor found itself drawn was to achieve a reputation for self-mastery and to outdistance his contemporaries in that field of competition. This normally great and hardly attainable prize was not such a difficult attainment in the Rome of the period, owing to the degenerate tendencies which then prevailed. The passions of society were divided between boy-sweethearts and mistresses, while many people gave themselves up to enter-

tainments, drinking parties, and all the extravagance
which these pleasures entailed — having picked up in a
trice, in the course of the war with Perseus, the vicious
proclivities of the Hellenes in these directions. So utterly
lost was the younger generation to all sense of decency
in the pursuit of these pleasures that it was a common
thing to have paid a whole talent for a boy or three hundred drachmas for a jar of Black Sea caviar. This movement aroused the indignation of Marcus Cato, who once
remarked, in a speech addressed to the Assembly, that
nothing revealed the degeneration of society so clearly
as the fact that handsome boys fetched more in the
market than real estate, and jars of caviar more than
livestock. This cult of pleasure flared out at the period
in question for two reasons: first, because the overthrow
of the Macedonian kingdom gave the Romans a sense of
now possessing uncontested world power; and, secondly,
because a lavish display of prosperity in private as well
as public life had resulted from the transport to Rome
of the treasures of Macedon. Scipio, however, set himself to realize the precisely opposite standard of behavior. He declared war upon all the lusts of the flesh;
and he molded his character and conduct into such complete harmony with themselves and complete agreement
with his principles that, in something like five years from
the start, he had established a national reputation for
self-command and self-mastery. . . .

Scipio had still to give attention to the virtue of cour-

age, which in any society — and especially in Rome —
is almost the fundamental virtue, and which therefore
demanded correspondingly vigorous cultivation. In this
endeavor, Scipio received a welcome piece of assistance
at the hands of chance. The Macedonian court had taken
the sport of hunting very seriously, and the nation had
reserved the most suitable parts of the country for the
preservation of game. These parks had been kept up as
carefully as ever during the whole duration of the war,
but had never been hunted over in these four years on
account of the preoccupations of the time, with the result
that they were teeming with all kinds of game. After the
war had reached a decision, Lucius Aemilius Paullus,
who considered that hunting was the best training as
well as the best amusement that a young man could have,
placed the royal huntsmen at Scipio's disposal and gave
him absolute authority in the hunting field. Scipio felt
like a king in his new domain and was absorbed in hunting for as long as the army remained in Macedon after
the battle. The intense enthusiasm for the sport with
which the young man was at that time inspired by the
coincidence of his age as well as his natural gifts in this
direction — in which he resembled a noble hound —
implanted in him a permanent taste. When he arrived
in Rome, he was fortified by finding that his enthusiasm
was shared by Polybius; and so it was that the time spent
by other young men upon the courts and upon social

functions, which tied them to the *piazza* in their efforts
to win popularity by the above-mentioned activities, was
spent by Scipio on the hunting field, where a constant
succession of brilliant and memorable feats secured him
a truer glory than any that was being won by his contemporaries. The others could not win praise except by
the injury of a fellow countryman — that being the normal consequence inherent in the nature of litigation —
whereas Scipio, without doing hurt to anybody whatso-
ever, was engaged in achieving a national reputation for
courage. It was a competition between words and deeds;
and the upshot was that in a short time he outdistanced
his contemporaries by greater lengths than any Roman
had been known to excel before his time — and this
though, in pursuit of glory, he took the opposite path to
everybody else in his treatment of Roman institutions
and conventions.

My excuse for enlarging upon Scipio's line of conduct
from his youth upwards is not only the belief that the
story will give pleasure to the old and bring profit to the
young, but more particularly the wish to prepare my
readers' minds to accept without incredulity what they
will read in regard to Scipio in succeeding volumes. I
wish to ensure that they shall not be perplexed by the
apparently extraordinary nature of some of the subse-
quent events in Scipio's life, and that they shall not rob
the hero himself of his deliberate achievements in order

to attribute them to chance. This they might be tempted to do through ignorance of the causes by which every event in his career is accounted for — the few events which have to be attributed to chance and fortuitousness being extremely limited in number.

CATO THE YOUNGER

CATO THE YOUNGER

(Marcus Porcius Cato)

95-46 B.C.

Translated from Plutarch, "Cato Minor," in *Parallel Lives*
(Teubner text, ed. C. Sintenis, Vol. IV), Chaps. 2, 65-70.

Cato the Younger

While Cato was still a child, the Italian confederates of Rome were agitating for admission to the Roman franchise, and Pompaedius Silo,[1] a gallant soldier and a very distinguished man, who was a personal friend of Drusus,[2] came to stay in the house for several days. During his visit, he made friends with the children, and said to them (playfully): "Look, won't you put in a word for us with your uncle to help us in our struggle for the franchise?"

Caepio [3] smiled and nodded assent; but Cato, instead of answering, glared defiantly into the visitors' faces.

"And *you,* young man," Pompaedius went on, "what have *you* to say to us? Don't you see your way to lend your visitors a hand in dealing with your uncle, as your brother does?"

---

[1] A citizen of the confederate canton of Marsica, afterwards commander-in-chief of the secessionists in the civil war of 90-81 B.C. [ED.]

[2] Marcus Livius Drusus, Cato's great-uncle on the maternal side and the Roman statesman who made the sincerest attempt to avert the imminent civil war by securing the franchise for the confederates constitutionally. The collapse of his policy, after his mysterious assassination, precipitated the catastrophe. Since the death of Cato's father, Cato himself, with his brother, sister, and half-sister, had been brought up in Drusus' household. [ED.]

[3] Cato's brother. [ED.]

Cato still said nothing, but his silence and his expression signified refusal; so Pompaedius picked him up, held him out of the window as though he were going to let him drop, and told him to say "Yes" or he would throw him out. As he did so, he put on a rough voice and kept on swinging the child's body, which he was balancing in his hands, from side to side out of the window. This went on for some time, but, when Pompaedius found Cato holding out nevertheless, without showing a trace of fear or intimidation, he set him down again gently and remarked to his friends: "What a piece of luck for Italy that this fellow is only a child! Had he been of man's estate, I don't believe we should have polled a single vote in the Assembly!"

＊　　＊　　＊

At the news that Caesar was actually on the march for Utica with all his forces [4] Cato exclaimed: "Look at that! Our friend realizes that we are men to be reckoned with!" Then, turning to the senators present, he urged them not to waste time but to look to their salvation while the cavalry were still there to cover them.

He proceeded to close all the town gates, except the

---

[4] In the Roman civil war of 49-45 B.C. between Gaius Julius Caesar and the constitutionalists, the last act but one was the campaign of 46 B.C. in northwest Africa, where Caesar's opponents had rallied their remaining forces. These had just been routed utterly at the Battle of Thapsus; and Utica (an autonomous town of Phoenician nationality, in which the constitutionalists had established their civil and military headquarters) was bound to fall. At Utica, at this moment, Cato was in command. [ED.]

gate leading to the shore (through which he organized
the evacuation)[5] — apportioning the ships to his officers,
keeping order, checking misconduct, composing brawls,
and providing ways and means for those who had none.
Meanwhile, Marcus Octavius encamped close to the
town with two legions and sent to Cato to insist upon the
demarcation of their respective commands. Cato, however, vouchsafed Octavius no answer, but remarked to
his friends: "Can we wonder any longer how our cause
has been lost when, with our feet on the edge of the
precipice, we see this officious spirit still rampant in our
midst?"

At that moment, it was reported to him that the cavalry
in retreat were beginning to plunder the Uticans' property as though they were in an enemy country. At once,
he ran after them at full speed, and took their loot away
from the first files which he encountered. The rest either
threw down or put down what they had taken before he
reached them, and the men were so ashamed that they
moved off in silence, without being able to look him in
the face. Next, Cato convened an assembly of the Uticans in town and put in a plea for the Three Hundred,[6]
begging his audience not to exasperate Caesar against
them, and suggesting that the two parties should co-
operate in working for their common salvation.

---

[5] There is a lacuna in the original Greek. [ED.]

[6] A provisional senate assembled at Utica by the constitutionalists, but recruited not so much from genuine senators as from
members of the local colony of Roman businessmen. [ED.]

Then he went back to the shore to inspect the progress of the embarkation and to say good-bye, as he saw them off, to any of his friends and acquaintances whom he could persuade to leave. His own son refused to take ship, and he did not feel justified in deterring him from standing by his father. There was a gentleman named Statilius who was young in years but who aspired to be strong-minded and to emulate Cato's imperturbability. Cato urged Statilius to sail — Statilius being a notorious anti-Caesarean — and, upon the young man's refusal, he caught the eye of Apollonides and Stoic and Demetrius the Peripatetic, and observed to them: "It is your business, now, to relieve this swollen head and readjust it to its true interests." His own time, during the whole of that night and the greater part of the following day, was occupied in helping to evacuate those who still remained and in giving his services to those who needed them.

Lucius Caesar, who was going to open negotiations on behalf of the Three Hundred with the other Caesar, his kinsman, came to beg Cato's assistance in working out a plausible line of defense to be used in pleading their cause — "though in pleading *your* cause," he added, "I should not be ashamed to go to the length of clasping Caesar's hand and falling at his knees."

Cato, however, told him not to think of doing so. "Had I wished," he explained, "to obtain salvation by grace of Caesar, I should have had to approach him in person and to deal with him man to man. It is not, however, my wish to be beholden to the tyrant on account of his illegalities — and an illegality it is that he should proffer salvation, like a lord and master, to those over whom he has no right to dominion. Begging off the Three Hundred is quite another matter, and this we will discuss together if you please."

After holding a consultation on the question with Lucius, Cato commended his son and his personal friends to the envoy's good offices, as the envoy started on his journey. As soon as Cato had seen him off and had bidden him farewell, he came back home, called together his son and friends, and gave them a long talk, in which incidentally he forbade the boy ever to touch politics. A career worthy of his own, he explained, was excluded henceforth by the political situation, and any other political career would be a disgrace.

Finally, toward evening, he went to his bath, and while he was taking it he suddenly thought of Statilius and shouted: "Apollonides! Apollonides! Have you brought Statilius down from his pedestal and got him away? Has the fellow actually sailed without saying good-bye to me?"

"Is it likely?" answered Apollonides. "We discussed it long enough, in all conscience, but his head is in the clouds and he is quite immovable. He declares that he will stay and do whatever *you* do."

At this, Cato is reported to have smiled and to have remarked: "That remains to be seen."

Having finished his bath he took dinner with a large company — sitting at table as was his habit after action.[7] Dining with him were all his personal friends as well as the members of the Utican municipal government. After dinner, over the wine, there was much engaging literary conversation. One philosophical theme circulated after another, until the discussion came round to the crucial Stoic paradoxes, "None but the good are free," and "All the bad are slaves." At that point, as was to be expected, the Peripatetic went into opposition, and then Cato fell upon him with might and main and went on and on in a voice harsh and vibrating with emotion. The extraordinary passion with which he spoke made it evident to everybody that he had resolved to put an end to his life as a way out of an impossible situation. For this reason the conclusion of his speech was received by all in a desponding silence, which led Cato to revive their spirits and divert their suspicions by once more raising questions and suggesting anxieties in regard to current events — enlarging upon his fears for the safety of their comrades at sea and their other comrades on the march across a savage and waterless desert.

On this note he broke up the party, went for his usual after-dinner stroll with his friends, and gave the necessary orders to the officers of the watch. As he was retir-

---

[7] Sitting, not *reclining*, which he never did except in sleep [AUTHOR.] At Hellenic dinner parties, it was usual to lie at full length on divans, instead of sitting up at table as is done by modern Westerners. [ED.]

ing, after this, to his own room, he once more aroused
suspicion by displaying less reserve and greater affection
towards his son and his various friends than had been his
way. However, he went in, lay down, and picked up
Plato's dialogue *On the Soul*. When he had run through
the greater part of the volume, he looked above his head
and found his sword missing from the place where it
should have been hanging,[8] whereupon he called a servant and asked him who had taken the weapon. Upon
the servant's remaining silent, Cato buried himself once
more in his book. But, after letting a few moments pass,
in order to give the impression that he was not in any
special hurry but was casually looking for the sword, he
ordered the servant to bring it. As the time passed and
nobody did bring it, Cato read to the end of the book
and then called again — this time summoning all the
household one by one and demanding the sword in a more
peremptory tone of voice. He went so far as to strike one
of them on the mouth with his fist, sufficiently hard to
draw blood from his own hand. By this time he was
angry and was shouting aloud that he was being betrayed, naked and defenseless, to the enemy by his son
and his servants, until finally his son rushed in, weeping,
with his friends, and flung his arms round his neck with
wailing and supplication.

At that Cato rose and looked him in the face with an

---

[8] His boy had removed it before Cato had risen from dinner.
[AUTHOR.]

expression of fury, in order to address him as follows: "Pray, when and where have I been mysteriously certified as being of unsound mind? — for that is how I am being treated. There is no attempt to argue me or to reason me out of what my friends are pleased to regard as a mistaken decision. I am simply denied the use of my own arguments and deprived of my arms. Why not tie up your father, sir, and have done with it? Why not pinion my hands behind my back until Caesar arrives to find me impotent even to defend myself? For attacking myself, after all, a sword is superfluous to me. If I want to kill myself, I have only to hold my breath for a little, or to strike my head just once against the wall."

At these words, the boy went out sobbing, and all the others with him except Demetrius and Apollonides, who remained behind and to whom Cato continued in gentler accents: "Well, are you, too, determined to keep a man of my age alive by compulsion and to sit here silently mounting guard? Or have you come with the story that there is nothing dreadful or disgraceful for Cato in waiting to obtain from the enemy the salvation which has failed him in every other quarter? If so, pray proceed. Convince me and convert me and thereby give me one reason more for being grateful to Caesar — as, no doubt, I must be if, all through him, I am to throw overboard the old beliefs and doctrines which have been my life-companions, and so increase in wisdom and stature. If you wish to know, I have not yet made up my mind in my own regard; but, when once I have done so, I must have the last word in executing my resolve. In a certain sense, I shall be making up my mind in consultation with you, since I shall be consulting those canons of reason which you yourselves employ in your philosophy. So please set your minds at rest and go back to my son with this message from me: He must not try to force upon his father what he cannot impose by persuasion."

To this speech Demetrius and his companion attempted no reply, but stole away in tears. The weapon was now sent to his room by the hands of a little boy; and, as soon as Cato received it, he drew it and examined it carefully. When he saw that the point was not turned and the edge not blunted, he said: "Now I am my own master"; after which he laid the sword aside and started to read his book again. Indeed, he is said to have gone through the whole work twice. After that, he went off into a sleep so profound that those outside the room were aware of it. Then, about midnight, he called two of his freedmen — Cleanthes the physician, and Butas, whom he employed as his principal private secretary. Butas he sent down to the shore, to ascertain whether everybody had left harbor and to report to him, while he allowed the doctor to bandage his hand, which had become inflamed as a result of the blow which he had struck the servant. This made everybody more cheerful, as a sign that life had not lost its hold upon him. Before long, Butas appeared with the news that all had left harbor with the exception of Crassus, who had been detained by some business but was now likewise on the point of embarking. He mentioned that the weather at sea was very stormy and that there was a great gale of wind. At this information, Cato groaned in pity for those on board ship and again sent Butas down to the shore, in case anyone might possibly have put back into harbor and be in want of necessaries— in which event Butas was to bring back particulars to him.

Although by this time the birds were singing, Cato again dozed off for a little. When, however, Butas returned with the report that in the harbor there was not a sign of life, his master ordered him to close the door and proceeded to stretch himself on his pallet as though he intended to spend the remainder of the night in repose; but Butas had no sooner left the room than Cato drew his sword and thrust it in below the ribs. Owing to the inflammation, he did not bring the full force of his hand to bear, and therefore failed to put an end to himself instantaneously. In his death agonies, he fell from the bed and knocked down a calculating machine standing by the bedside with a crash which set the servants shrieking and brought his son and friends into the room in a moment. They saw Cato bathed in blood, with the greater part of his intestines protruding, yet with life still in his body and light in his eye. Although the shock to all was terrible, the doctor found, on approaching, that the intestines had escaped perforation, so he attempted to replace them and to sew up the wound. The moment, however, that Cato came to himself and recovered consciousness, he pushed the doctor away, tore the wound open again, mangled his intestines with his hands, and died.

Index